COLONIAL PEOPLE

The Schoolmaster

WIL MARA

 **Marshall Cavendish**
Benchmark
New York

Other Marshall Cavendish Offices:
Marshall Cavendish International (Asia) Private Limited, 1 New Industrial Road, Singapore 536196 • Marshall Cavendish International (Thailand) Co Ltd. 253 Asoke, 12th Flr, Sukhumvit 21 Road, Klongtoey Nua, Wattana, Bangkok 10110, Thailand • Marshall Cavendish (Malaysia) Sdn Bhd, Times Subang, Lot 46, Subang Hi-Tech Industrial Park, Batu Tiga, 40000 Shah Alam, Selangor Darul Ehsan, Malaysia

Marshall Cavendish is a trademark of Times Publishing Limited

All websites were available and accurate when this book was sent to press.

Library of Congress Cataloging-in-Publication Data

Mara, Wil.
The schoolmaster / by Wil Mara.
p. cm. — (Colonial people)
Includes bibliographical references and index.
Summary: "Explore the life of a colonial schoolmaster and his importance to the community, as well as everyday life, responsibilities, and social practices during that time"—Provided by publisher.
ISBN 978-0-7614-4801-3
1. Teachers—United States—History—Colonial period, ca. 1600–1775—Juvenile literature. 2. Schools—United States—History—Colonial period, ca. 1600–1775—Juvenile literature I. Title.
LA215.M37 2010
371.100973—dc22
2009029690

Editor: Christine Florie
Publisher: Michelle Bisson
Art Director: Anahid Hamparian
Series Designer: Kay Petronio

Expert reader: Professor Paul Douglas Newman, Ph.D., Department of History, University of Pittsburgh, Johnstown

Photo research by Marybeth Kavanagh

Cover photo by The Granger Collection, NY

The photographs in this book are used by permission and through the courtesy of: *The Bridgeman Art Library*: Yale University Art Gallery, New Haven, CT, USA, 4; New Walk Museum, Leicester City Museum Service, UK, 14; Josef Mensing Gallery, Hamm-Rhynern, Germany, 21; *North Wind Picture Archives*: 7, 22, 23, 36; *The Image Works Archives*: 9, 17; ARPL/HIP, 29; *Corbis*: Gianni Dagli Orti, 13; Bettmann, 33; *The Granger Collection, New York*: 19, 30, 39; *The Colonial Williamsburg Foundation*: 28

Printed in Malaysia (T)
1 3 5 6 4 2

CONTENTS

ONE   The Colonial Period in America 5

TWO   The Schoolmaster 11

THREE   Colonial Schools 18

FOUR   A Typical School Day 25

FIVE   Schoolmasters and the
Colonial Community 34

Glossary 42

Find Out More 44

Index 46

ONE

The Colonial Period in America

In the mid– to late sixteenth century, ships sailed from Europe to North America carrying thousands of people from different countries. Many wanted to escape terrible living conditions in Europe, which included the threat of being punished for their religious beliefs. There was also little hope of ever making good money. Some came at the request of various European businesses that hoped to profit from the rich lands of the New World. Still others were brought over as servants and laborers, often against their will. They all gathered together in small groups, bringing along their cultures and customs. They settled in territories, called colonies, which were under the control of European monarchs and nobles.

The Pilgrims landed at Plymouth, Massachusetts, in 1620. Some hoped to find religious freedom, others wealth.

The risks of coming to America were huge. First, there was the voyage across the rough seas. Colonial ships could also be overcrowded. If one person got sick, everyone got sick and some would die. Those who did manage to reach America had to get busy building homes and growing food. Cutting down trees was hard work, but the wood was needed for building, and the land had to be cleared to plant crops. Diseases were also common, and there were very few medicines and even fewer doctors. Many colonists died from illnesses that are easy to cure today. Others were killed by American Indians.

Too Busy for School

Since every day was a struggle to survive, schooling was the last thing on a colonist's mind. If you were a slave or an **indentured servant**, you never even considered the possibility of getting an education. Children were often too busy to think about schooling. Their labor was just as important to keeping a house or farm running as that of the adults. Children and teens planted seeds, fed animals, cooked meals, and mended clothes. All these chores left very little time for anything else. What little learning they did get was thanks to their parents. Even then, they learned only what they needed in order to do more work.

Some colonial children had to help run their family's home and farm, leaving no time for school.

In the late 1600s and early 1700s **missionaries** began introducing various faiths to colonists who were not already followers of a religion. Soon these people wanted to teach their beliefs to their children. They, as well as parents who already belonged to a religion, knew that this instruction would be easier if the children could read the Bible and other religious books. It was not long before the adult colonists realized the need for schools.

Schools Arrive in the Colonies

The Massachusetts colony was the first to build schools. In 1642 a law was passed that said all parents who did not teach their children to read and write risked having to pay a fine. In 1647 a second law said that every town with fifty or more homes had to have an **elementary school** teacher, and every town with over a hundred homes had to have a **grammar school**. The nearby colony of New Haven, in what is now Connecticut, wrote a law of their own in 1650 that used the same ideas as the Massachusetts laws. Religious leaders controlled all parts of school life, from what was taught to who would be hired to teach.

Soon there were schools being built throughout the colonies. By the mid–1700s schools taught less about religion and more of general subjects. All through the seventeenth century, the colonies of Rhode Island and Maryland did not require that schoolmasters have religious backgrounds. In many areas, there were very few students, or teachers, either, and so no one bothered to make such demands.

Parents were also beginning to realize that their children would improve their chances for the future if their schooling went beyond religion. If a young boy learned arithmetic, for example, he might one day run his own business. If he also developed good reading,

The Boston Latin School

The oldest school in the United States is the Boston Latin School, located in Boston, Massachusetts. It was founded on April 23, 1635, and is still open today. It began with fewer than ten students, all of them young boys from wealthy families. The list of famous people who have gone to Boston Latin includes Benjamin Franklin and four other signers of the Declaration of Independence. Many Boston Latin students went on to Harvard, America's first college, which was founded one year later.

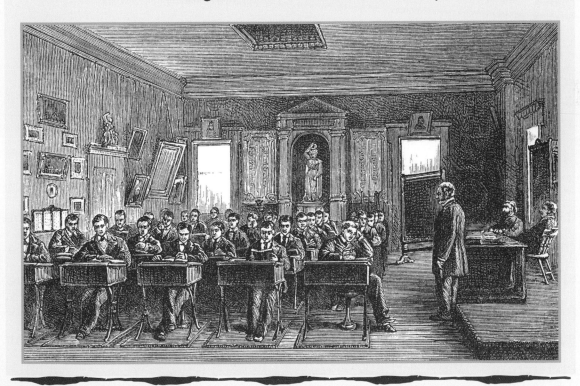

writing, and speaking skills, he could become a member of a town's government. Wealthy families did not need their children to work around the house or on the property; they had servants and laborers for that. Instead, privileged children were expected to get an education and uphold the family's high position. The great majority of students in all schools were boys, for girls were not treated equally in colonial society. It was felt that their place was in the home, where the duties did not require formal schooling.

The importance of an education was humorously presented in this poem, which was popular in colonial times.

> *He who ne'er learns his ABC*
> *Forever will a blockhead be*
> *But try to learn, be wise, and then,*
> *You will be lov'd by all good men.*

There were many types of schools when the colonial period came to an end in July 1776. Some were for general learning, others prepared youngsters for college, and a few taught a specific trade such as carpentry or blacksmithing. And the most important person in each school, to be sure, was the schoolmaster. He prepared America's young boys for whatever challenges awaited them.

TWO

The Schoolmaster

Teaching youngsters could be difficult and challenging in colonial times. Many schoolmasters had to be more than just teachers. They also had to act like police, judges, inventors, ministers, and friends. Many created their own lessons from scratch. Passing knowledge to young students in a country where public schooling was in its early stages of development was not easy.

The Colonial Schoolmaster

Colonial schoolmasters came from all walks of life. Many had a college education; others had made it through only a few years of elementary school. There were towns in colonial America where it was difficult to find anyone willing to take a schoolmaster's job, usually because the pay was so low. Sometimes a schoolmaster taught part time. In his other job, he might be a minister, physician, lawyer, **artisan**, shopkeeper, or farmer. Women who taught often also served as cooks, maids, or housekeepers.

Most colonial schoolmasters, however, were men. During the colonial period men were recognized as the authority figures in every area of life. They made all the decisions regarding their family, their business, and their town. It seemed only natural, then, that men would also be in charge of education. They were thought to be better at keeping order, as children were usually more fearful of men than women. Also, many colonial women were themselves uneducated, so they were not considered able to teach. A few schoolmasters were indentured servants. The owner of a servant who could teach would rent the servant out and take a portion of his or her pay.

Some schoolmasters taught privately, teaching just one or two students at a time. For example, if a wealthy man wanted his son to learn silversmithing, he might pay a silversmith to teach the boy. Or, the man might hire a schoolmaster to teach his children basic subjects, but with greater attention than would be possible in a school where there were other students. Teaching privately was a good way for schoolmasters to earn extra money. Sometimes classes were held at night, on Saturdays, or at times of the year when the schoolmaster's regular school might be closed.

In colonial America many men took on decision-making responsibilities and areas of importance in everyday life. They were put in charge of education as well.

The Look of a Colonial Schoolmaster

Many schoolmasters were older men. They were often described as having long, gray hair (or wigs that looked roughly the same) and clean-shaven faces. They wore three-cornered hats, long coats, button-down vests, and shirts with frilled cuffs. White silk socks were pulled to the knees, and their leather shoes had large buckles. Some also wore silk ties or kerchiefs that were formed into bows, and they might carry a walking stick or a cane. Small round glasses occasionally completed the picture.

Qualifications

Not everyone in colonial times could become a schoolmaster. You had to meet a certain set of qualifications, or traits and characteristics that enabled you to do the job. However, the qualifications in one town might be very different from those in another. Also, qualifications changed as time went on.

In the early years of the colonial era, a schoolmaster's two most important qualifications were a strong religious background and solid character. Accordingly, he had to have a deep understanding of the religion he was to teach, plus a good reputation as a person. For example, a man who did not attend religious services every Sunday had little hope of becoming a schoolmaster. The same was true of someone who had a habit of breaking the law, such as drinking too much or using bad language in public. In 1654 a Massachusetts court said schoolmasters should not "have manifested themselves unsound in the faith, or scandalous in their lives." Sometimes a person had to get a license before he could teach in a religious school.

As time passed and schools concentrated less on religion, a schoolmaster's knowledge of common academic subjects became more important. People who had graduated from college had the easiest time getting a schoolmaster's job. When it came to teaching in grammar schools—where young boys learned classical languages so they could go to college—a schoolmaster had to have a college education. In an elementary school, on the other hand, anyone who knew the basics of reading, writing, arithmetic, and a few other subjects had a good chance of becoming a schoolmaster.

A Schoolmaster's Pay

Pay was one of the least attractive parts of the schoolmaster's job. Generally, a schoolmaster did not make very much money. Because of this, it was often very hard to get a talented man to take the job. Young men who had been to college, for example, usually wanted work that earned more.

Of those who did want to become schoolmasters, some were forced to take second jobs. This was especially true in areas where most of the families were poor and could not afford to pay a schoolmaster in money. Instead, he'd be given useful goods such as wheat, grain, fruits, vegetables, meat, cider, beer, or wood for building or fuel. This was part of a system called bartering, in which people simply traded for the things they needed, with no money involved. A schoolmaster might also receive a valuable service, such as that of a blacksmith or a carpenter. Towns that wanted to hire good schoolmasters but did not have much money for wages might offer a free home and some land. A schoolmaster might also live with a family while he gave lessons to the children. During his stay, the family provided food and a place to sleep.

The money for a schoolmaster's pay—if he received any pay at all—could come from many places. Sometimes the source was **taxes**. At other times subscriptions were raised. These were contributions, usually from wealthy people who lived nearby.

Sometimes schoolmasters were not paid with money. Instead, they were provided a service, or food and a place to live.

Some of the subscribers did not even have children, but they still felt strongly about the importance of having a school in their community. Then there was tuition—money paid directly from the students' parents to the schoolmaster. Tuition was common in schools that had been started by the schoolmaster, who then ran it as a business. Only the best schoolmasters could hope to receive tuition, and the parents expected their children to get an excellent education.

THREE

Colonial Schools

The schools of colonial times were quite different from those of today. It wouldn't be until the mid–1800s when towns across America developed a common approach to education.

Schools of Different Types

The type of school you attended was determined by many things. Where you lived, how much you or your town was willing to spend on schooling, and what you wanted to do once your schooling was over were all considered.

The colonial school most similar to the schools of today usually went by one of three names—elementary, **primary**, or **petty**. "Elementary" was probably the most common. Students were anywhere from ages two or three to thirteen or fourteen. Elementary schools taught subjects such as reading, writing, spelling, and arithmetic (also called ciphering), plus some religion. In later years, elementary students were given lessons in bookkeeping, surveying, literature, art, history, music, and even dance. Many colonial children never received more than an elementary education.

A second type of colonial school was called a grammar school. Today, grammar schools and elementary schools are basically the same thing. In colonial times, however, a grammar school prepared its students (almost always young boys) for college. That meant

Colonial elementary schools included students as young as two or three and as old as fourteen.

learning two languages—Greek and Latin, which were taught not just through memorizing and repeating words and phrases, but also by reading Greek and Latin books.

Educational institutions of yet another type were known as **academy schools**. These varied widely. One in Massachusetts might teach Latin and Greek, just like a grammar school. Another in Pennsylvania might teach mostly math or reading and writing. Yet another might specialize in woodworking or farming. Author Lawrence Cremin, in his book *American Education: The Colonial Experience, 1607–1783*, gives a broad definition: "Perhaps the most that can be said of any given academy is that it offered what its master was prepared to teach, or what its students were prepared to learn, or what its sponsors were prepared to support, or some combination or compromise among the three."

The Schoolhouse

Before there were school buildings, children received an education anywhere they could. Many people think of a colonial school as a little red building with a bell ringing from a steeple. But classes could be held anywhere—a church or meetinghouse, a manse (the local minister's residence), a shop, an inn, someone's home, even a barn or a shed. Most towns did not have enough money to build

The Dame School

Dame schools were very much the same as elementary schools as far as subjects were concerned. The difference is that the schoolmaster was a woman (*dame* is short for *madame*), and classes were held in her house. Attending dame school was a good way for children to get an education in a town that did not offer any other schooling. The best dame schoolmasters were those who were educated themselves. Many were not, and so their schools were little more than daycare centers. But educated women with small classes could do a wonderful job of teaching.

schools. At best, classes might be held in an empty building that had been used for something else. Sometimes schoolmasters traveled from town to town, teaching in whatever location was available. Classes meeting under this arrangement were said to be part of the system of **moving schools**.

Even when a school was built from scratch, it did not look like the schools of today. Early colonial schools were simple one-room log cabins with mud and stones stuffed between the logs to keep out bad weather. Square holes cut through the logs served as windows. Glass, however, was rare back then. Instead, the holes were often

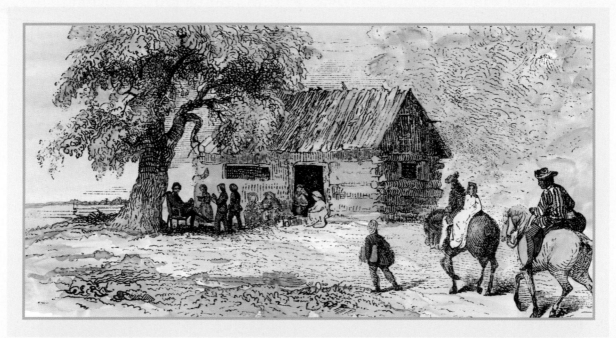

Some schools in early colonial America were one-room log cabins. Students arrived either on foot or by horseback.

covered with sheets of heavy paper coated with oil or lard that would let sunlight come through. The floors were either bare earth or wooden boards. The roof was made from more boards or, sometimes, plain logs, often with hay or bark tied down to provide extra cover.

Light was provided by candles or oil lamps. During the winter, warmth came from a fireplace. This usually stood at the back of the room. It was built either from wood or large stones, and held together with clay. It was not unusual for smoke to

Rows of cut logs served as desks in early colonial schools.

drift out of the fireplace during class and stain the ceiling with soot. Children usually sat on rows of long benches in the middle of the classroom. Narrow tables stood in front of them to act as desks. A few clever schoolmasters created desk space by cutting holes into the log walls, inserting long logs (so they stuck out a foot or so), then setting narrow planks across the logs. As time went on, the quality of school furniture improved.

Paper, like glass, was fairly expensive in colonial times. For this reason, some children learned to write on tree bark. The bark from birch trees, in particular, actually worked very well. Tiles of slate were also used as a crude type of writing tablet. Pens and pencils were often unavailable, so children wrote with a rough stick of graphite or a **quill**. The pointy end of the quill was cut at a sharp angle to create a sharp tip. The tip was dipped into a small bottle of ink and could be used to write for a line or two before the student had to dip it again. Even if children provided their own feathers, it was the schoolmaster who did the cutting.

The schoolmaster had a large table at the front of the room, plus a chair or a bench. Some also had a lectern—a stand with a slanted top—from which to deliver lessons. If a schoolmaster wanted to write something down for his students to see, he had no blackboard, whiteboard, smartboard, or markerboard. Instead, he would use a large slate tile or a piece of paper or bark that was then passed around the room.

FOUR

A Typical School Day

A typical school day in colonial times was, in some ways, very similar to a school day in the twenty-first century. An elementary school day could last anywhere from three to eight hours depending on the age and gender of the students, and on how many students there were. Grammar schools could start as early as 6:00 AM and go straight until 4:00 or 5:00 PM. Most colonial schoolchildren got a break at lunch, including time to eat plus a recess period when they were allowed to play.

In the Mornings

Getting to school in colonial times often meant walking. If a child lived in farm country, where the homes were spaced far apart, a walk to school could take up to an hour or more. Because of the long walks, it was not unusual for some children to arrive much earlier than others. When this happened, a schoolmaster might give the early arrivals quiet work to do—such as reading a book—until the class filled up. Some wealthy children got to school on horseback or in buggies. A few lucky students did not need to walk or ride at all—their lessons took place in their own homes.

On the coldest mornings children were sometimes asked to bring wood for the fireplace. This was because a schoolmaster could not be expected to provide enough firewood for a whole winter. With everything else he had to do—making lessons, reading papers, sharpening quills, and so on—he hardly had time to chop wood every day. A student who forgot to bring wood might be told to go home and return with a log or two.

A schoolmaster often began the day with a prayer. Sometimes this would be followed with a **hymn** that the class sang together. The students could recite their prayers and hymns from a book, but doing it from memory always made their schoolmaster proud.

Subjects

The subjects taught in colonial times varied from school to school. However, the four that were most common were known as the "Four Rs": reading, 'riting (writing), 'rithmetic (arithmetic), and religion. The teaching of religion was known as catechism.

Morning Inspection

Upon arriving in the morning, students were likely to be inspected by the schoolmaster. Being clean and healthy was very important in colonial days. Diseases were common, and one sick child could easily spread the illness to an entire class. Some schoolmasters also did not want to see dirty hands, faces, or clothes. They felt it was their duty to teach the children the importance of being clean. Many youngsters were sent home to wash up before they could take part in lessons.

Religion was taught by denomination—Methodist, Roman Catholic, Baptist, and Quaker were among the Christian denominations present in America during colonial times. As more families moved into a town, it became difficult for a schoolmaster to teach for just one denomination. Some schoolmasters tried to solve this problem by teaching general catechism, but this approach seldom worked. Parents wanted their children to learn the exact religion they followed. A schoolmaster would also teach the Ten Commandments from the Bible, asking the students not only to memorize them but also to explain what each one meant.

There were several other subjects commonly taught beyond the "Four Rs." Handwriting was one. While it was important for a youngster to spell correctly, it was also important to write in a neat and readable way. Writing was the only way people had to communicate with each other aside from speaking, so having good penmanship was a valuable accomplishment. Many schoolmasters also taught smart everyday habits such as being organized, polite, and thoughtful, managing money well, and using time wisely.

In this re-created schoolhouse in Colonial Williamsburg, Virginia, a boy practices his handwriting. Quills and ink wells were used instead of the pens and pencils that are common today.

Teaching Methods

Teaching was fairly simple in colonial times. The schoolmaster would stand or sit at the front of the room and talk. The students would then be expected to write down or memorize each lesson. Some schoolmasters would repeat a lesson over and over, then make his students do the same. This so-called **rote** method could be very boring. A few days after a lesson, each student had to come to the front of the room and repeat what he had learned, then be graded.

Some schoolmasters tried to make the lessons fun. One way to do this was to use little songs or rhymes. A common rhyme from colonial times went like this

Thirty days hath September,
April, June, and November;
Of twenty-eight there is but one,
And all the rest have thirty-one.

This little rhyme taught students how many days were in each month of the year, and it is still used in schools today.

A student recites a lesson to his schoolmaster.

In schools with large classes, a schoolmaster might ask some of the older students to teach the younger ones. He would give an older child a lesson, then test the younger students later on to see how much they had learned.

Books were costly in colonial America. Hornbooks were used in their place.

Books

Books were rare and very expensive in colonial times. Most were brought over from Europe on ships carrying other supplies. They became more common by the late 1600s when colonists had printing presses of their own.

One book that many students used was called a **psalter**. It was mostly for religious lessons, as it contained religious poems or hymns (psalms), plus other religious material. Another educational tool was the **hornbook**. In spite of the name, a hornbook was more like a paddle on which a sheet of paper was pasted bearing important information, such as multiplication tables or the letters of the alphabet. The paper was protected by a thin sheet of transparent

Make Your Own Hornbook

This is a quick and simple way to make something similar to the hornbooks used by schoolchildren in colonial times.

Things You Will Need
- A piece of large, sturdy cardboard
- Glue or paste
- A sheet of plain paper
- A sheet of clear plastic wrap
- A pair of scissors (ask for an adult's help if they are too sharp)

Instructions:

1. On a piece of cardboard, draw a paddle shape and cut it out. (If you have a Ping-Pong paddle lying around, feel free to use that.)

2. Cut a piece of paper to fit over the paddle.

3. Write your favorite school lesson on the paper (such as the letters of the alphabet, multiplication tables, or state capitals). Paste the paper onto the paddle.

4. Use a piece of clear plastic wrap to cover your hornbook. This will be like the animal horn covering the colonial students used. You can tape it around back if necessary.

5. Done! Bring it into school and surprise your teachers!

horn, which was much tougher than paper because it came from the horn of various animals. Perhaps the most common schoolbook in colonial times was *The New England Primer*, first published in 1690. It was mainly used to teach reading, but it did so through religious lessons. It contained hymns, poems, and many illustrations.

Punishments . . . and Rewards

A colonial schoolmaster was usually quick to punish his students for bad behavior. In fact, a schoolmaster was expected to use punishments when necessary. At the same time, however, the best schoolmasters knew how to reward their students for good behavior and hard work.

A child who misbehaved might be asked to sit at the back of the classroom. Students who were good would then sit up front. This made children want to sit as close to the front as possible. Another method of punishment was to have a child stand at the front of the classroom wearing a **dunce cap** before all the other students. This was embarrassing, and very few students wanted to go through the ordeal twice. Another way to punish a student through embarrassment was to have the other students yell something insulting at him, for example, "Lazy, lazy, lazy!" If a student kept forgetting a lesson, he might be asked to try it again—while kneeling on a hard floor.

Some schoolmasters punished students physically, usually by hitting. The punishment itself could be a light slap on the head, or a twisted nose or a pulled ear. But it might also be much harsher, like cracking the knuckles with a ruler, smacking the back with a wooden rod, or—perhaps worst of all—delivering a whipping.

The best colonial schoolmasters knew how important it was to reward their students for good behavior. They might give little gifts or special privileges. A favorite reward among students was having their names written on a piece of paper and hung on the wall. A child who did something else well might get a check next to his or her name. The schoolmasters who are remembered with the greatest fondness, it seems, are those who used kindness and good humor rather than cruelty.

A common punishment for misbehaving in a colonial schoolhouse was to wear a dunce cap in front of the class.

FIVE

Schoolmasters and the Colonial Community

Schoolmasters found different opportunities in different colonial towns. People in some places were more religious than others. New England colonists, for example, were mostly Puritans, which meant that they tried to live a very pure life in God's eyes. One northern schoolmaster said that the purpose of teaching was to show how, "a Christian must set his steps to grow daily and increase in understanding and life." Some towns had many families and therefore many students, whereas others had very few. In poor communities, a schoolmaster might not be paid enough to survive by teaching alone. Also, some towns did not feel that the teaching of the "Four Rs," or formal schooling, was as important for their children as learning a trade or working at home.

Schools from One Community to the Next

Formal schooling started in the northern colonies and grew quickly in the same area. New England had many schools by the late 1600s and early 1700s, including elementary schools, grammar schools, and colleges. The first college in America, now known as Harvard University, began in Massachusetts as Harvard College in 1636. On the other hand, the southern colonies were the slowest in developing school systems. Many towns were **plantation** communities. Families lived far apart from each other, which made it difficult to build a school that all children could easily get to.

Schools of certain types were more common in certain areas. In towns with large populations, you were more likely to see grammar schools and colleges. The farther you got into the country, the more elementary schools you would find. In farm country, dame schools were common, as were moving schools. A youngster who lived in a farm area but dreamed of going to college might have a tough time getting there.

By the mid–1700s schools were being built all over America, including in the southern colonies. A child who went to school had a much better chance of being successful in all areas of life. A young man with a college education would likely find

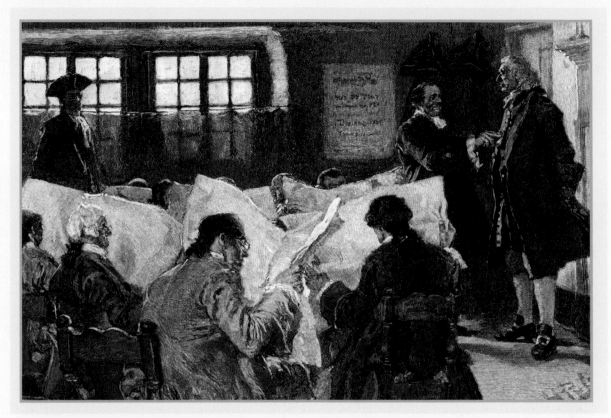

As colonial America grew and sought independence from England, the ability to read and write became ever more important.

a job that paid well. Also, it was more important than ever to know how to read. America was printing its own books and newspapers by this time, and a person needed to know what was happening in the colonies. As the demand for schools grew, so did opportunities for people to become schoolmasters. By the time America declared its independence from Great Britain in 1776, being a schoolmaster was a good job.

The Cost of Starting a School

Schools were not cheap to build and maintain. In the early colonial days, most people were more concerned with building their own homes and clearing land for farming. Eventually, however, it became necessary to put the same kind of effort into providing a place for children to learn.

Money to build schools came from several different places. One source of funds consisted of wealthy people. Every now and then a town in need of a school would discover that someone had passed away and willed the town enough money to build a new schoolhouse. Or, the town might be given an abandoned building, a house or a barn, plus the land it was on. Sometimes a kindly person made a gift of supplies such as firewood, farm animals, or an orchard full of fruit trees.

In some areas, even if there was not much money available, the people of a town still found a way to get a school up and running. As a group, the townspeople might choose a plot of land, clear it off, then build the schoolhouse together. Then they would all contribute something to keep it going. A farmer might give extra food, a carpenter would build benches and tables, and so on. In this way, a town could have a school without spending a lot of money.

Students of All Kinds

The great majority of schoolchildren in colonial times were white boys. In spite of this, there were some differences between them. In the early days of the colonial era, many had only recently come from countries other than England. That meant that they, as well as their parents and anyone else who lived in their homes, still spoke the language of their native European country. This sometimes made it difficult for schoolmasters to teach in English, and the children from Holland, France, or other countries had to learn English as they went along. Some children ended up speaking two languages—one at school and another at home. This also explains why many student papers that have survived from the colonial era have unusual spellings—the children spelled some words in the English way and others according to another language.

American Indians and African Americans were sometimes seen in colonial schools. Many colonists made the attempt to include American Indians in the growing public education system, teaching them not only reading, writing, and arithmetic, but also their basic religious beliefs. African Americans, on the other hand, were kept as slaves during this period, and many believed that slaves did not need to learn much beyond farm work. Some slave owners did hire schoolmasters to give their slaves lessons on an elementary level.

But for the most part, African Americans saw very little education during the colonial days.

A child's education was also decided by how much money his family had. Poor families, at best, might be able to send their children to an elementary school. Anything beyond that could be very expensive. A schoolmaster who came to someone's home to teach children privately, for example, expected to be well paid for his time.

Some slave owners hired schoolmasters to educate their slaves. This however, did not happen very often.

Christopher Dock—A Life in Service to His Community

Christopher Dock devoted most of his adult life to teaching the students of his Pennsylvania community. Born in Germany, he came to America in about 1714 and settled in the town of Skippack. Aside from ten unhappy years spent as a farmer, Dock taught until his death in 1771. He was known for his gentle kindness and love of his students. His way of teaching was so effective that several books were written about him. He once said that a, "poor beggar child, **scurfy**, ragged and lousy, if he has a disposition to learn, should be as dear to the schoolmaster though he never receive a penny for it in this world."

Conclusion

The schoolmaster was one of the most important figures in colonial history. He sometimes had to work under the most difficult conditions—crowded, uncomfortable classrooms, uncertain salary, lack of supplies—and often for very little pay. He taught everything from reading, writing, and arithmetic to the importance of religion, good manners, and personal responsibility. Sometimes he had to hand out punishment, but he preferred to give rewards instead. Without schoolmasters to guide America's colonial children, the nation could not have become what it is today.

Glossary

academy school   a type of school in colonial times; lessons varied from place to place, often based on what the schoolmaster chose

artisan   a skilled craftsperson

dame school   an informal school where the schoolmaster was a woman and taught the same basic subjects as an elementary school, but in her home

dunce cap   cone-shaped hat that students had to wear as punishment

elementary school   the most basic type of school, where general subjects such as reading, writing, and arithmetic were taught

grammar school   a school that prepared young boys for college

horn   a tough, transparent material made from the horns of various animals

hornbook   a paddle-shaped object with a lesson sheet attached on one side

hymn   a religious song

indentured servant   a person under contract to work, without pay, in exchange for passage to a new country

missionary   a person sent to a territory to do religious work

moving school	a type of school that was served by a schoolmaster who traveled from town to town, teaching children in whatever place was available
petty school	another name for an elementary school
plantation	a very large farm property
primary school	another name for an elementary school
psalter	a schoolbook designed to teach religious lessons, usually through hymns and religious verses
quill	a large bird feather (often the wing or tail feather of a goose) that was used for writing.
rote	to learn through repetition and memory
scurfy	skin that is dry and flaky
taxes	money collected from people who live in a town, state, or country

Find Out More

BOOKS

Hazen, Walter. *Colonial Times.* Tucson, AZ: Good Year Books, 2008.

Johnson, Terri (compiler). *What Really Happened in Colonial Times.* Mississauga, ON, Canada: Knowledge Quest Books, 2007.

Kalman, Bobby. *A Visual Dictionary of a Colonial Community.* New York: Crabtree Publishing, 2008.

Roberts, Russell. *Life in Colonial America.* Hockessin, DE: Mitchell Lane Publishers, 2007.

Stewart, Toby. *Colonial Teachers.* New York: PowerKids Press, 2005.

DVDs

Desperate Crossing: The Untold Story of the Mayflower. Los Angeles, CA: A&E Home Video, 2006.

Liberty's Kids: The Complete Series. Los Angeles, CA: Shout! Factory, 2009.

WEBSITES

Social Studies for Kids

www.socialstudiesforkids.com/subjects/colonialtimes.htm

This site provides information on the life and times of colonial America. It has many excellent links.

Kid Info

www.kidinfo.com/American_History/Colonization_Colonial_Life.html

The Kid Info page on colonial life features many excellent links and much useful information.

Kids Zone

www.history.org/kids/games/

The games and activities page from the Colonial Williamsburg site has many fun and interesting things to do, all with educational value.

Index

Page numbers in **boldface** are illustrations.

academic knowledge, 15–16

academy schools, 20

African Americans, 38–39, **39**

American Education: The Colonial Experience, 1607–1783, 20

appearance of teachers, 14, **14**

attitudes toward schooling, 6–8, 10

backgrounds for teaching, 11–12

bartering, 16

books, 30, 32, 36

Boston Latin School, 9, **9**

children, 6–10

Colonial Williamsburg, Virginia, **28**

colonists, **4**, 5–6

communities, 34–36

cost of schools, 37

Cremin, Lawrence, 20

dame schools, 21, **21**

desks and furniture, 23, **23**

Dock, Christopher, 40

dunce cap, 32, **33**

education, 6–10

elementary schools, 18–19, **19**

girls, 10

grammar school, 19–20

handwriting, 28

Harvard University, 35

hornbook, **30**, 30–32

income, 16–17

men, 12

missionaries, 7

money for schools, 37

morning inspection, 27

moving schools, 22

The New England Primer, 32

newspapers, 36

paper and tablets, 24

pay, 16–17

printing presses, 36

private teachers, 12, 39

psalter, 30

punishments, 32–33, **33**

qualifications to teach, 15–16

quills, 24

religion, 27

religious knowledge, 15

religious leaders, 8

religious persecution, 5

rewards, 32–33, **33**

rhymes/poems, 10, 29

school day, 25–33

schoolhouses, 20, **22,** 22–24, 37

slaves, 38–39, **39**

students, 38–39

subjects, 26–28

taxes, 17

teaching methods, 29–30, 40

trade, 16

traits and characteristics, 15–16

tuition, 17

types of schools, 10, 18–24

wages, 16–17

wealthy families, 9, 10, 12

women, 12

writing tools, 24

About the Author

Wil Mara has written more than a hundred books, many of which are educational titles for young readers. A full bibliography of his work can be found at www.wilmara.com.